RELIGIONS TO
INSPIRE

for KS3

Hinduism

Jan Hayes

Series editor: Steve Clarke

DYNAMIC LEARNING

HODDER
EDUCATION
AN HACHETTE UK COMPANY

The Authors and Publishers would like to thank Seeta Lakhani for advising them on the content of this book.

The Publishers would like to thank the following for permission to reproduce copyright material:

Photo credits
p.5 © Paul Almasy/Corbis; **p.9** © UTOPIA – Fotolia; **p.12** © curved_horizon – Fotolia **p.13** © Jan Hayes; **p.14** *t* © Hemant Mehta/India Picture/Corbis, *b* © Jan Hayes; **p.15** © Geray Sweeney/Corbis; **pp.16–17** © Steve Vidler/Alamy; **p.18** © Photononstop/SuperStock; **p.20** © World Religions Photo Library/Alamy; **p.24** © Frederic Soltan/Sygma/Corbis; **pp.26–27** © Lindsay Hebberd/Corbis; **p.30** © Ajay Verma/Reuters/Corbis; **p.31** © Frederic Soltan/Corbis; **p.33** © Pedro Ugarte/AFP/Getty Images; **pp.34–35** © supertramp88 – Fotolia; **p.36** © World History Archive/TopFoto; **p.37** © Art Directors & TRIP/Alamy; **p.40** *t* © Art Directors & TRIP/Alamy, *b* © Angelo Giampiccolo – Fotolia; **p.47** © Julian Kumar/Corbis; **p.49** © NASA; **p.50** © AP/Press Association Images; **p.51** *t* © AP/Press Association Images, *b* © Phil Noble/Reuters/Corbis; **pp.52–53** © Stapleton Collection/Corbis; **p.55** © The Print Collector/Alamy; **p.56** © Najlah Feanny/Corbis; **p.61** © Juliet Ferguson/Alamy; **p.62** © Louise Batalla Duran/Alamy; **p.63** © Jan Hayes; **p.64** © Darren Brode – Fotolia; **p.66** © Hipix/Alamy; **pp.68–69** © Narinder Nanu/AFP/Getty Images.

Acknowledgements
p.23 www.hinduism.co.za/sacramen.htm#4 for the quote from the Griha Sutra; **p.42** quote from the *Bhagavad Gita*, published in 1972 by the Bhaktivedanta Swami Prabhupada; **p.46** www.hinduwebsite.com/sacredscripts/rigintro.asp for the quote from the Rig Veda; **p.60** subknow.reonline.org.uk/node/91 for the quote from the Sri Ramakrishna; **pp.61–62** www.bbc.co.uk/schools/gcsebitesize/rs/environment/histewardshiprev1.shtml for the quotes from the Mahabarata; **p.61** www.chitralakshana.com/trees.html for the quotes from the Varaha Purana.

Every effort has been made to trace all copyright holders, but if any have been inadvertently overlooked the Publishers will be pleased to make the necessary arrangements at the first opportunity.

Although every effort has been made to ensure that website addresses are correct at time of going to press, Hodder Education cannot be held responsible for the content of any website mentioned in this book. It is sometimes possible to find a relocated web page by typing in the address of the home page for a website in the URL window of your browser.

Hachette UK's policy is to use papers that are natural, renewable and recyclable products and made from wood grown in sustainable forests. The logging and manufacturing processes are expected to conform to the environmental regulations of the country of origin.

Orders: please contact Bookpoint Ltd, 130 Milton Park, Abingdon, Oxon OX14 4SB. Telephone: (44) 01235 827720. Fax: (44) 01235 400454. Lines are open 9.00–5.00, Monday to Saturday, with a 24-hour message answering service. Visit our website at www.hoddereducation.co.uk

© Jan Hayes 2012
First published in 2012 by
Hodder Education
An Hachette UK Company
Carmelite House, 50 Victoria Embankment
London EC4Y 0DZ

Impression number   5
Year   2016

Cover photo © Oytun Karadayi/iStockphoto.com
Illustrations by Barking Dog Art, Peter Lubach, Oxford Designers & Illustrators Ltd, Tony Randell
Typeset in Minion regular 12.5pt/15pt by Wooden Ark
Printed in Dubai

A catalogue record for this title is available from the British Library

ISBN: 978 1444 12222 0

Contents

1.1 Where did Hinduism begin?

Learning objectives

You will ...
- find out about where Hinduism began
- understand how Hinduism began
- evaluate the impact of where and how it began on the development of the religion.

'Where did Hinduism begin?' is a very difficult question to answer and even among Hindus there is disagreement. It started in a very different way to some of the other religions you might study.

It probably started about four or five thousand years ago with the river people who lived in the Indus Valley. Their traditions developed into the Hindu faith (though some people disagree with this).

Unlike other religions, Hinduism was not started or inspired by a single person.

The word Hindu was probably first used to refer to the people who lived across the River Indus.

The collection of beliefs, traditions and practices we call Hinduism began in the north of India.

The British used the word Hinduism to describe the religion practised by Indian people who were not Jews, Christians or Muslims.

In India, people practise their religion in different ways: for example, some **festivals** are celebrated only in certain parts of India.

Its teachings were spread by word of mouth, because few people could read at this time in history, so there was no single place where it started.

The religion has developed from a variety of different cultures, beliefs, teachings and traditions over time.

Many Hindus refer to their faith as '**Sanathan Dharma**', which means eternal spiritual path: it has no beginning and no end.

Map labels: Islamabad, PAKISTAN, River Indus, Delhi, Jaipur, Agra, Lucknow, NEPAL, BHUTAN, River Ganges, BANGLADESH, Ahmedabad, INDIA, Kolkata, Mumbai, Pune, Hyderabad, Bangalore, Chennai

Remains of an old ruined city by the River Indus. Much of the River Indus is now in modern Pakistan.

Knowledge check

1 Where did Hinduism probably start?

2 Roughly how long ago did Hinduism begin to develop?

3 Which people are believed to have begun the religion of Hinduism?

4 What phrase do Hindus sometimes use as a name for their faith?

Activity A

1 Using a blank map of India, label the main cities. Colour the route of the River Indus in blue.

2 Find out the name and location of five famous Hindu temples. Make sure they are not all in the same part of India.

Activity B

Find out about five famous Hindu temples. Research the temples and find a picture and three facts about each one.

Activity C

Imagine a Hindu was coming to your school. You will have a chance to ask questions about their religion.

1 Design a set of five questions to ask them about their religion.

2 Conduct an investigation to find out the answers to your questions.

Activity D

'Hinduism is a religion of the unknown.'

1 What do you think of this idea? Why do you think someone might say that? Think about the ideas on pages 4–5 to help you.

2 Explain the reasons why you agree or disagree with that statement.

1.2 What are the Hindu holy books?

Learning objectives

You will ...
- find out about the variety of Hindu scriptures
- understand the differences between Shruti and Smriti
- know examples of each type of text
- compare texts that come from God with texts that help us understand the words of God.

Hindu scriptures

All religions have special books that contain their teachings: Christians have the Bible, Muslims have the Qur'an, and so on.

However, when we look more closely, we find some holy books are actually collections of books. The Christian Bible, for example, is a collection of 66 different books.

Sometimes, it is difficult for people to understand the deep meanings of their special books, and they may need help to apply the teachings in their daily lives. For example, as well as the Qur'an, Muslims have the Hadith, a collection of sayings and stories about Prophet Muhammad that helps explain the Qur'an.

Hinduism, too, has many holy books. They can be divided into two kinds: **Shruti** and **Smriti**.

Each of these is split into many parts – so there are many Hindu holy books.

There are so many books that people argue about which are more important. They were all originally spoken and not written down. As time went on people learnt by heart what they had heard and then later they were written as books.

Many books were written in the ancient Sanskrit language which some Hindus today cannot understand at all. Hindus today use their priests to help them translate and therefore understand them.

Knowledge check

Read pages 6–9.

1 How many kinds of holy books are there in Hinduism?

2 What are they called?

3 In which language are they written?

4 How do people today understand the ancient texts?

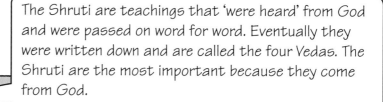

So what does Shruti mean? Can you explain it simply for me?

The Shruti are teachings that 'were heard' from God and were passed on word for word. Eventually they were written down and are called the four Vedas. The Shruti are the most important because they come from God.

So really they are the words of God. The Shruti tell us about God-like 'revelations' and cannot be changed, much like the Qur'an.

OK, so what are the Smriti then?

Well, the Smriti are teachings that 'were remembered' from what ordinary people had been told about God. They are not the word of God. They are man-made texts.

In a way they help people to understand and apply the Shruti today – just as the Hadith helps Muslims understand the Qur'an. They are more well known by people.

OK, so ... for a Hindu, you have to have the Shruti – the word of God – because that's where it all starts, but some people will say that the Smriti makes the truths and teachings more understandable. They are updated for a modern world so they are always relevant. The Hindu scriptures are a collection of different types of books.

Shruti

The Shruti scriptures are called **Vedas** and are books of knowledge. They are used during worship, at special occasions that mark important events in life, and at religious celebrations.

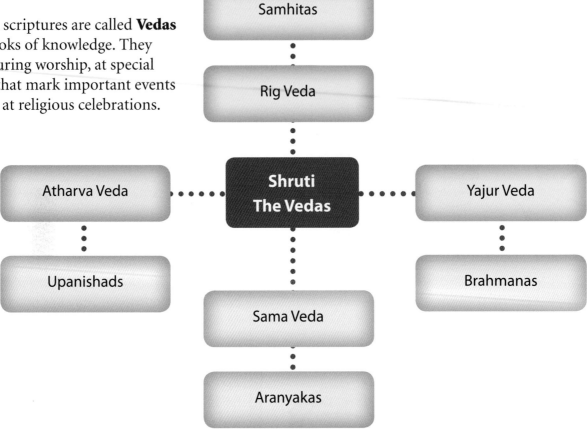

Smriti

The Smriti contain historic and legendary tales which are written in story form. The stories provide religious teachings, often in picture form.

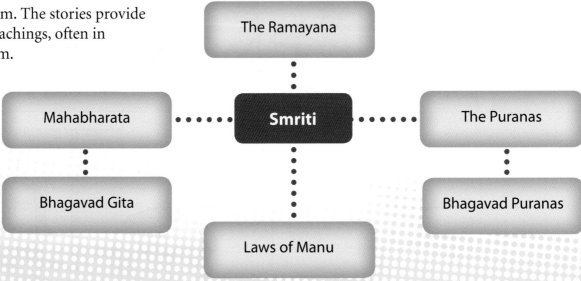

Reading scriptures from holy books during early morning prayer in a temple in the northern Indian city of Amritsar.

Activity A

Make a fact chart about Hindu scriptures using information from pages 6–8.

Activity B

Choose one of the Hindu holy books. Research what the book is about and design a front cover that shows what you would find inside it.

Activity C

Find out about and explain in detail the difference between Shruti and Smriti. You could draw up a table of comparisons.

Activity D

What do you think is more important – a book that is believed to contain the words of God or a book written by humans that explains the words of God? Discuss your answer with a classmate.

1.3 What is the Ramayana?

Learning objectives

You will ...
- find out about the story of the Ramayana
- understand the morals involved in the story
- understand the lessons for life that Hindus can learn from the story.

The **Ramayana** is an **epic** story written across seven books and it tells the story of **Rama**. It is a story well known and well loved by all Hindus.

The Ramayana is a moral story in which Hindus are given valuable lessons for life. In the story of Rama and **Sita**, Hindus can learn about the values of loyalty, courage, respect for elders, obedience and keeping promises.

The characters' lives tell of the duties of a good father, son, brother, wife and king. This serves as a reminder of the right ways to behave. It tells us that there is evil in the world and that our bad choices can lead to serious consequences. At the same time though it gives Hindus hope that good will always overcome evil.

The Ramayana story is told on page 11.

Knowledge check

Read pages 10–11.

1. What is the Ramayana?
2. Who is the story about?
3. What morals can be learnt from the story?
4. What hope does this story give Hindus today?

Activity A

In groups of four, write a play/script that tells the story of Rama and Sita.

Activity B

Read the cartoon on page 11 separately and then in pairs. For each character, write down the good and the bad qualities that they show.

Activity C

Identify and explain the motives behind the way each character behaves in the story.

Activity D

1. Imagine you are in court. How would you defend the following against the given charges?
   - The queen (for tricking Rama out of the throne and for trying to get her own son, Bharata, to be king).
   - **Ravana** (for deceit and kidnap).
2. Write your defence statement for each.

Dasaratha, the king, was growing old and wanted to name his successor.

He chose his eldest son, Rama, but the evil queen wanted her son, Bharata, to be king instead.

The king kept his promise to grant the queen a wish because she had saved his life earlier.

The queen's son became king and Rama was sent out of the kingdom for fourteen years.

However, the queen's son refused to be crowned king and placed Rama's slippers on the throne till he returned.

Rama, Sita his wife and Lakshmana his brother lived in the forest for fourteen years.

Rama and Lakshmana went out hunting and left Sita in a protective magic circle.

Sita was tricked out of the magic circle by a begging holy man.

The holy man was really Ravana, the ten-headed demon god, who took Sita prisoner in his castle on the island of Lanka.

Rama and Lakshmana, helped by Hanuman, the monkey god, and his army of monkeys, made a bridge to the island of Lanka.

A big battle took place and Ravana was killed by an arrow from Rama.

Rama and Sita were welcomed home and Rama was crowned king. Oil lamps were lit everywhere.

1.4 What do you find in a Hindu temple?

Learning objectives

You will ...
- know that a Hindu temple is called a mandir
- find out what a temple looks like inside and out
- understand the meanings and uses of the items in the mandir.

Below is an example of the outside of a **mandir** (also known as a temple). A mandir is believed to be the home of God.

You will notice the carvings and images on the entrance to the temple. These are usually images of the **deities** (gods) associated with that temple.

The main **shrine** is called a **garbha griha**. It is opposite the door and found on the farthest wall. It is the place that contains the statues of the main deities that the mandir is dedicated to. There might be two or three statues in it. You would see the statues painted and garlands of flowers hung over them. These garlands are given by the worshippers. There will also be food and flower offerings, all of which are gifts from the worshippers to the deities.

Side shrines are found on the side walls of the mandir. They have smaller statues which will also have offerings of food, flowers and coloured powders around them.

This is an **arti** tray. It is used for a particular part of worship which takes place many times in a day. The priest lights the lamp and worshippers pass their hands through the flame and then touch their foreheads as a blessing from God.

Holy water is called Charanamrita. It is the water that is left after the statues have been washed and bathed. Worshippers sprinkle it on themselves after praying as a kind of blessing.

All shrines have a bell. It is rung to show worshippers are ready to worship and symbolically to awaken the deities in the shrine.

Each temple has its own priest(s). All priests come from the Brahmin **caste**. Their job is based in the temple taking offerings, giving blessings, looking after the deities, and explaining teachings from the scriptures.

Knowledge check

1 List the things you would find in a mandir.
2 Describe what you would see at the main shrine.
3 Why is a bell needed in a temple?

Activity A

Look at pages 12 and 13. With a classmate, write down ten things you notice or questions you would want to ask about the images.

Activity B

Look at pages 12 and 13. What interesting or unusual things did you notice about the images? What questions did you want answered? Through a class discussion, can you come up with any answers to these questions?

The **Aum** symbol is thought to be the sound of the universe being created. It is pronounced Om. It is special to Hindus for whom it means 'God and Everything that is'. Worshippers often meditate using this word by repeating it over and over.

Popular symbols like these are found in temples. The **swastika** is thought to bring good fortune.

Activity C

Imagine that you run a company that provides tours to places of worship. You have been asked to create a tour guide sheet for a Hindu temple. It should include a picture and text to help the tourists learn about the mandir.

Activity D

The mandir is a highly decorated building. What are the advantages and disadvantages if a holy building is highly decorated? Give reasons for your answers, and examples to help you explain. Think about this in terms of a worshipper, and a non-worshipper.

1.5 How do Hindus worship?

Learning objectives

You will …
- know the different kinds of worship in which Hindus may participate
- learn how a Hindu carries out worship in the mandir and the role of the shrine in family worship
- understand and evaluate the importance of the mandir in the daily life of a Hindu
- analyse the importance of the home in comparison to the mandir for Hindu worship.

When Hindus worship, they believe that they make direct contact with God (**Brahman**) through a deity.

Although many Hindus worship at home (at their family home shrine), the main acts of worship, festivals and special occasions in family life are celebrated in the mandir. Many Hindus visit the mandir daily to make offerings, take blessings, offer prayers and to listen to hymns and teachings. Many visit very early in the morning and others in the evening after work. Dawn and dusk are considered good times to worship, as this is when the world is calm and peaceful.

Early morning I carry out **puja** first at home. Later on, before going to work I visit the mandir for **darshan**. I ring the bell on entering the temple and offer my respects to the **murti**.

I pray to ask God to be with me during the day, sort of to protect me. I also donate some money into the offerings box. I take some **prasad** from the priest and drink some holy water. I see believers doing **parikram** and **japa**.

At weekends sometimes my family and I go to the mandir really early for arti. We join in the **kirtan** and **bhajan**. We watch the priest dress the murti and then offer **havan**. The priest can be seen giving out blessings and accepting offerings from the worshippers.

arti greeting ceremony with a lamp

bhajan and **kirtan** hymns and chants

darshan seeing the deity or holy person

havan sacred fire ceremony

japa meditation/prayer

murti image of God which helps worship

parikram circling of the shrine

prasad offering and eating sacred food

puja worship

pravachan talk about the Hindu scriptures

sewa service to the deity or holy people

Worshipping in a mandir

The arti ceremony

Hindus believe that everything in the universe is made up of five elements. They are earth, water, fire, air and ether (space). They are represented in the arti ceremony with five lamps.

- Carrying out the arti ceremony is the way Hindus show their love for and devotion to God. In return they receive blessings from the deity.
- The arti tray (see page 14) has an oil lamp on it, so it is often called the 'ceremony of lights'. The ceremony starts and ends with the blowing of a conch shell filled with water. Flowers and offerings which represent the earth are given to the murtis, and a fan is often waved to symbolise the air. At the same time the bell is rung and people meditate facing the deities.
- The arti lamp represents the fire element; it is waved in front of the deities. This gives it their power and blessings. The worshippers pass their fingers over the flame of the arti lamp and touch their foreheads to take on the power.
- Some offerings are given back to the worshippers and water is sprinkled over their heads.

Havan

- Havan is a sacred fire to which ghee, camphor, wood, grains and seeds are offered.
- The priest purifies himself with holy water. The priest performs this act of cleansing by holding a bowl in his left hand, into which he dips a finger and touches his ears, nose, mouth, arms, body and legs.
- Worshippers do the same. Sacred sounds are chanted as the grains are thrown into the fire.

An arti ceremony.

Bhajan and kirtan

- Bhajan means 'adoration' and kirtan means 'glorification'. Bhajans are songs (hymns) and kirtan is the chanting of mantras.
- Hymns are sung either in small groups or by the whole congregation. Kirtan is the repeating of mantras (sacred sounds, words or phrases) to the beat of the music. Both kinds of worship are used in the arti ceremonies.

Darshan

- Darshan is when worshippers present themselves in the temple to the murti/deity. It is like having an 'audience' with someone special. They are paying respects and receive blessings through the priests.
- They bow their head and cross their arms. Some will prostrate themselves (lie full length on the floor) in total respect of God.
- They make offerings, which could be money, fruit, flowers, etc. Many Hindus 'take darshan' at the mandir before work. They sip holy water, take prasad and often take part in the arti as well.

Prayer and meditation

- It is quite common to see people sitting in a quiet corner of the mandir praying and meditating.
- They might meditate using mantras ('Om namah shivaya' being a popular one). They might use 'mala' (prayer beads) to help them focus on prayers. These actions are done to purify their hearts, to make them less selfish and to take on the love of God.

Sewa

- Many Hindus offer sewa (service) to the mandir. This might include cleaning, cooking temple food, offering food collected in the mandir to the poor.
- The priests themselves are also involved in service, not only by leading worship but also by helping the wider community.

Knowledge check

1 What items are used in the arti ceremony?

2 Why is arti important?

3 When do most Hindus go to the temple (mandir)?

4 Explain what sewa is.

Worship at home

(1) Worship (puja) is carried out at the family shrine. This might be in a special room in the house or more likely in the corner of a room. The shrine will be a small statue or murti of the family god and several pictures of other Hindu gods.

(2) The murtis come in many forms, but Hindus still worship Brahman, the one true God, when they worship them. **Ganesha** (the elephant god) is a popular murti for families to have because he symbolises good fortune which comes from God.

(3) The room is cleaned and the mother of the house will shower and put on clean clothes before she prays.

(4) The shrine has a range of statues and pictures/images of various murtis. An arti tray will also be on the shrine.

(10) She and her family are now ready to face the day ahead.

(9) The arti lamp is lit and waved in front of the murti. The mother then places her hands over the lamp, passes her hands over her eyes and then over her head.

(5) The mother pours water over the murti and it is then 'dressed' with garlands and clothes.

(8) Often a tray of fresh fruit is offered. This reminds the worshippers that all things come from God and they should remember to thank God for them.

(6) The mother then puts a spot of coloured paste between the eyes of the murti, on her own forehead and on the family members that are present. She then prays in front of the shrine. She lets her mind be still and focuses on God.

(7) She now makes offerings – usually of flower petals and lighted incense sticks.

My name is Raksha and I have three children. My husband goes to work very early in the morning and he often calls at the mandir to offer worship. I lead the worship for my children at our special shrine.

It is not very big or expensive but it is a really special place for our family. We have a small statue of Ganesha and even smaller ones of **Lakshmi** and **Krishna**. We also have several photos of other deities. To me they help remind me of Brahman and help me understand about God more clearly. Some people say it's idol worship but they are very wrong. These statues represent qualities of the One God. They remind me of his power, creation, wisdom, help, love but also his ability to destroy.

My aim is to give God my respect, to ask God to help me focus for the day, help me deal with things in a calm way and to treat people around me with love and respect.

Activity A

Rewrite the speech bubble on page 17. Change the key words (in bold) by giving an explanation of what the words mean. Use the definitions on page 17 to help you.

Activity B

Design a story board showing puja being done in the home.

1 Use eight boxes. Decide what you are going to include in each of your eight boxes before you begin to draw/write. Use the information on page 20 to help you.

2 Underneath each picture/image in the text box, write down why you think these actions are being done or what the worshipper is showing by doing such actions. How do you think people feel after taking part in morning puja in the home?

Activity C

Design an information booklet/leaflet explaining what happens in a Hindu mandir. Use a variety of images and written information.

Activity D

Compare worship in the home with worship in the mandir.

1 Explain the similarities and differences. You will need to describe these, as well as explaining their symbolism.

2 Which do you think is more valuable to a believer? Explain your answer. You might want to refer to your own or another religion in your answer.

1.6 How do Hindus mark important stages in life?

Learning objectives

You will ...
- learn about the events and symbolism surrounding birth and childhood in Hinduism
- understand the symbolism of wearing the Sacred Thread for Hindu boys
- learn about how **karma** is linked to teaching children good moral values.

In Hinduism rites of passage are very important. These are the important stages of life and are called **samskaras**. There are sixteen. They start from before birth, with parents deciding when is the right time to have a child, and run through life until death.

Birth and childhood

Let's look at what happens when a child is born into a Hindu family. Concern for the well-being of the child begins even before it is born. A couple who are thinking of starting a family will often consult their temple priest to find out when the best time would be to actually have the child. Many Hindus visit a Hindu astrologer for a reading of their child's fortune.

Some of the sixteen samskaras related to birth.

Birth

When the child is born, Hindus carry out little ceremonies as directed by their holy books.

- A letter of the Sanskrit alphabet is decided by the date and time of the baby's birth. The baby is then given a name starting with that letter.
- The symbol for Aum is drawn on the baby's tongue in honey. This is in the hope that it will be a sweet-natured child.
- Many Hindus shave the baby's head or ask a priest to shave its head. In some parts of India, the whole family will have their heads shaved. The hair represents the past lives of the person (Hindus believe in **reincarnation**, which means the **soul**/spirit lives through many lifetimes). Shaving the head is like cutting away the actions from the past life, and making a new start.

The Griha Sutra says:

'When a baby is born the father should come to see it. He should bathe and put on clean clothes. He should then offer prayers to God. Holding the child in his lap he should turn to the east and using a gold ring put a few drops of honey and ghee in the baby's mouth. He should say "I give you this honey which comes from God the creator of the world. May God protect you, may you become strong and firm like a rock, an axe for the wicked and bright in character. May God give you long life and understanding of the Vedas."'

Why do you think Hindus have these rituals before the baby can even understand them? Well, the idea is to have God there from even before the start of life and with the child from the moment of birth.

Hindus believe that if a child has the idea of God and the teachings of the holy books at the centre of its life as it grows up, then it will make the right moral choices when faced with dilemmas.

Naming the child

- This should be done on the eleventh or twelfth day after birth.
- Before noon, the father completes an act of worship helped by the family priest. He spreads rice grains on a metal plate and writes the chosen name in the rice with a gold ring.
- A prayer is said so that the child will be clever, healthy and obedient to his duties.

Hair-cutting

The first haircut.

- After its first birthday the child has its hair cut.
- On the day of the shaving, the family makes an offering of ghee and wood fuel to the god of fire. They fill four pots with rice, barley, pulses and sesame, and place them near the fire.
- The child sits in front of his father, and is faced by the barber who then shaves his head with a razor. The baby's nails are also trimmed.
- These actions show their hope for cleanliness, good health and long life for the child.

Ear-piercing

Ear-piercing is done for both boys and girls in the hope that the child will receive the blessings of a long and healthy life.

Summary

After all these rituals it is believed that God will look after the child. Hindus believe God will guide the child to make the right decisions and choices. They will be brought up to value the religious teachings.

Knowledge check

Read pages 22–27.
1 What do Hindus call the sixteen stages of life?
2 What happens before the birth of a child?
3 What do Hindus do to try to make sure the child will be sweet-natured?
4 Why do Hindus think God will look after their child?

The Sacred Thread Ceremony

The tenth samskara is the upanayana which means 'getting close to God'. It is better known as the **Sacred Thread Ceremony**.

Hindus believe that going through any of the samskara ceremonies purifies the soul. This is probably the first ceremony which the child is old enough to really understand.

The Sacred Thread is a very proud moment for families because at this point the boy becomes 'twice born', and can now carry out his religious duties. His first birth was when he was actually born and the second is this one where he is accepted into his religious class (**varna**).

From this point on his religious teacher is like a father and the religious teachings are like a mother to him. He is now seen as responsible enough to take on his spiritual life and duties.

Traditionally this was a ceremony only for boys, but today in some communities girls also have the ceremony. There is no reason in the holy books why it is only a boy's ceremony; it just has been that way in Indian history.

The three duties

A **duty** is something a person has to do. It is like a debt they owe and in this case the boy now has this debt of duty throughout his life.

1 The first duty is to Brahman.	2 The second duty is to his ancestors.

3 And the third duty is to his spiritual/religious teacher.

Traditionally the boy would move from his family to the care of his spiritual leader, living in an ashram, which is like a community set up to develop and train people in a religious life. He would learn values and be educated through the study of the holy books. This happens rarely today.

This ceremony for a boy takes place between the ages of eight and twelve. Other religions have similar ceremonies – for example, Confirmation in Christianity or Bar Mitzvah in Judaism.

What happens at the ceremony?

The ceremony follows a pattern of actions that will affect the boy for the rest of his life. Leading up to the day of the ceremony, special family feasts will be held. Then on the day of the ceremony, the house is decorated (often with flowers), and there is more feasting.

- First the boy has his head shaved; he bathes and puts on new clothes. It is a special day and like a new clean start. The boy and his father make offerings to the deities at their home shrine in the morning before the ceremony takes place.

- The ceremony can take place at home but more commonly it happens at the temple because it is easier to light the havan (fire) there. The fire symbolises that God is present and acts as the eternal witness to the ceremony.

- At the temple the boy is given wheat, rice and small amounts of silver and gold by his mother and other relatives, which he passes to the **Guru**, his religious teacher. The boy also places a garland of flowers around the neck of his Guru. He sits on the left of his Guru. His hands are covered with a cloth. Drums are beaten and conch shells are blown. The Guru whispers something to the boy which remains a secret.

- The boy is stripped to his waist like the priests and the thread is placed over his left shoulder. He then listens to the **Gayatri mantra** being said. This is a special religious prayer. He may be given a new spiritual name, to show this new start, and his second birth.

- He takes vows (promises) to study the Vedas, serve his teachers and follow certain rules in his life. He promises to try to always be pure in thought, words and actions.

- From now on, at dawn, noon and dusk every day, he will wrap the thread around his right thumb and repeat that prayer.

- He gets a new thread every year, putting the new one on before he takes the old one off. He will wear a thread all his life.

- The ceremony finishes with the boy giving the Guru a gift.

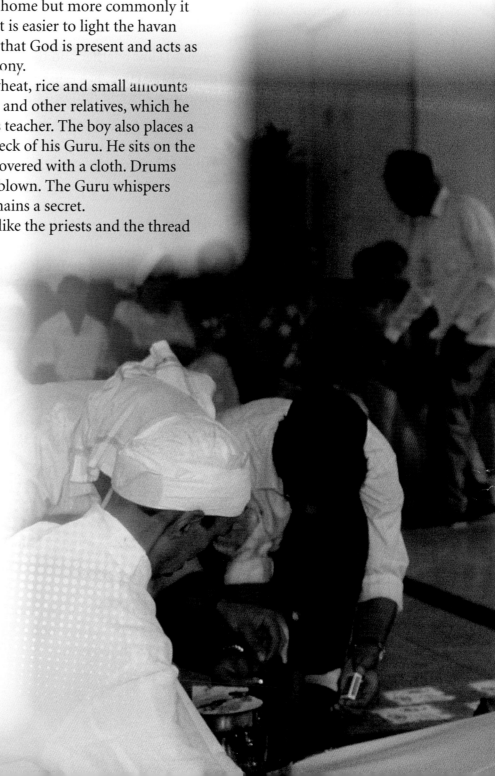

The importance of the thread

The thread is sometimes made of three long strands of different coloured cotton – each of these is itself three threads. The nine threads represent nine deities, who can help in a person's life. The three strands represent three stages of life (student, householder and retiree) and also three sacred fires. A special knot ties the threads together.

The boy has now made a *commitment* to his religion and he has taken *vows*, which are promises that he has to keep. One promise is to study because education is the key to his future. His thoughts, words and actions should be *pure* so that he leads a good life. He is now an adult and so he must take responsibility for his behaviour.

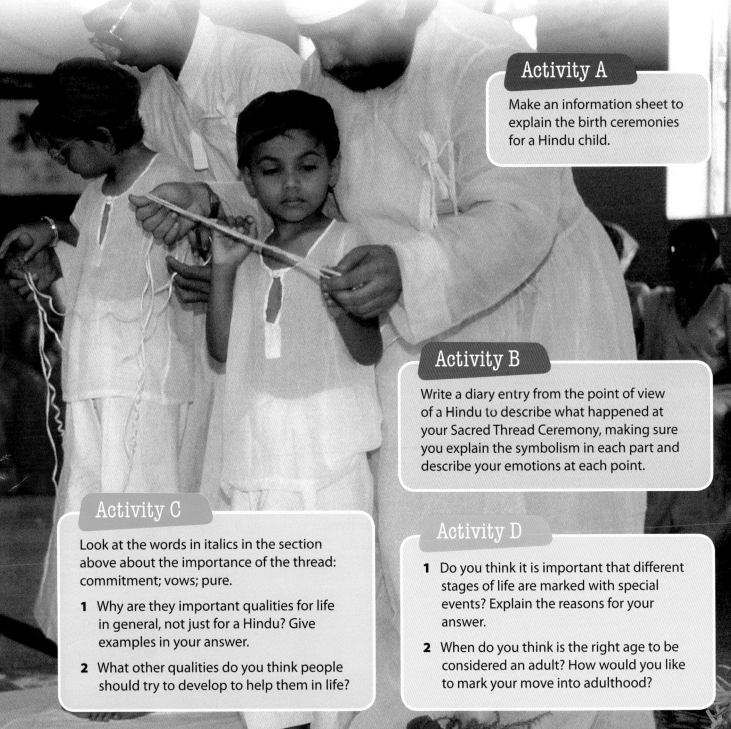

Activity A

Make an information sheet to explain the birth ceremonies for a Hindu child.

Activity B

Write a diary entry from the point of view of a Hindu to describe what happened at your Sacred Thread Ceremony, making sure you explain the symbolism in each part and describe your emotions at each point.

Activity C

Look at the words in italics in the section above about the importance of the thread: commitment; vows; pure.

1 Why are they important qualities for life in general, not just for a Hindu? Give examples in your answer.

2 What other qualities do you think people should try to develop to help them in life?

Activity D

1 Do you think it is important that different stages of life are marked with special events? Explain the reasons for your answer.

2 When do you think is the right age to be considered an adult? How would you like to mark your move into adulthood?

1.7 What festivals do Hindus celebrate?

Learning objectives

You will ...
- find out about what is meant by a festival
- understand the celebration and meaning of two key Hindu festivals
- analyse the link between Hindu festivals and pilgrimage.

Festivals are times of celebration. There is a great variety of festivals that are celebrated in Hinduism. Because Hinduism is a collection of different traditions, not all Hindus celebrate the same ones. The festivals that a Hindu celebrates will depend on the tradition they follow and which part of India they come from.

The festivals remember stories from Hindu scriptures. They remember the stories of the Hindu gods and goddesses. These are sometimes called epics, like the stories in the Ramayana for example (see pages 10–11). Other festivals can remember events in the lives of a holy person or they might be seasonal festivals, for example the spring festival of **Holi**.

Festivals are important for the following reasons:
- They are special times that bring families and communities together in celebration. Often work places and schools shut so that families can be together.
- They are joyful occasions with special foods, parties, new clothes, etc.
- They have a serious side – the stories have important religious and moral teachings. They help people understand the scriptures better. They often act as a reminder or a guide for Hindu life today; for example, the idea of good overcoming negative forces and the choices people make in their lives.
- They can inspire people to continue to worship and do religious duties.

Knowledge check

Read pages 28–33.

1 What is a festival?

2 What do Hindu festivals remember?

3 Why are festivals important for the family?

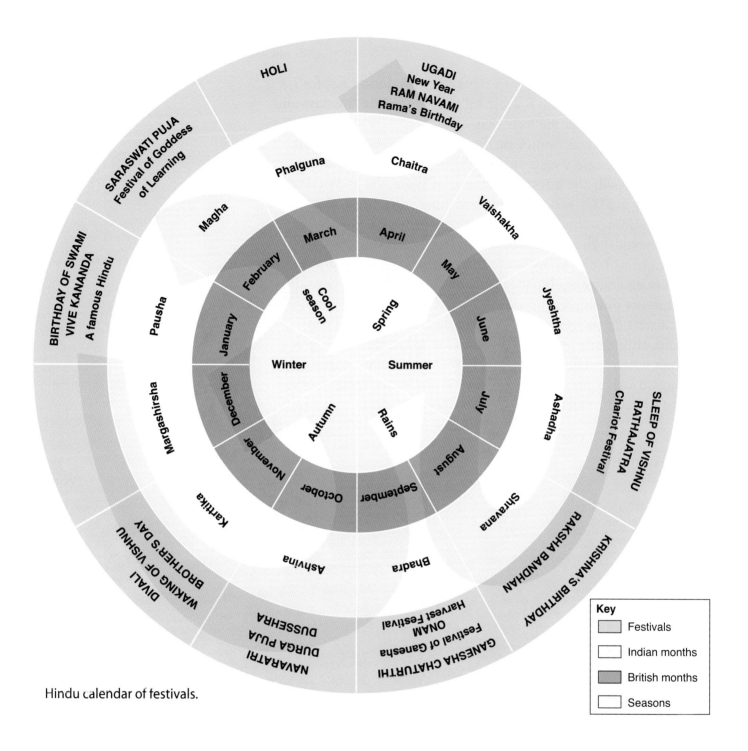

Hindu calendar of festivals.

Key
- Festivals
- Indian months
- British months
- Seasons

Festivals shown on the wheel:

HOLI

UGADI New Year RAM NAVAMI Rama's Birthday

SARASWATI PUJA Festival of Goddess of Learning

BIRTHDAY OF SWAMI VIVE KANANDA A famous Hindu

SLEEP OF VISHNU RATHAJATRA Chariot Festival

DIVALI WAKING OF VISHNU BROTHER'S DAY

NAVARATRI DURGA PUJA DUSSEHRA

GANESHA CHATURTHI Festival of Ganesha ONAM Harvest Festival

KRISHNA'S BIRTHDAY RAKSHA BANDHAN

Indian months: Phalguna, Chaitra, Vaishakha, Jyeshtha, Ashadha, Shravana, Bhadra, Ashvina, Kartika, Margashirsha, Pausha, Magha

British months: March, April, May, June, July, August, September, October, November, December, January, February

Seasons: Spring, Summer, Rains, Autumn, Winter, Cool season

Activity A

Choose one of the festivals, and answer these questions about it:

1 Name the festival you have chosen.

2 What does this festival remember?

3 How is this festival celebrated?

Activity B

1 Design a postcard for a Hindu festival.

2 One side should be images of the festival. The other side should be a description of how that festival is celebrated today and the background to those celebrations.

3 Describe the celebrations as if you were part of them.

Diwali

Diwali celebrates the Ramayana. This story is told in Chapter 1.3 (see pages 10–11). Diwali is a festival of lights lasting five days and for many it celebrates the New Year.

- Before the festival, homes are decorated and new clothes, oil lamps, foods and sweets are bought and made. Lamps are placed outside the houses in honour of Yama, the god of death.
- The day is a family day including visiting, gifts, fireworks and celebrations.
- The next day the goddess of good fortune, Lakshmi, is the focus of worship. Many lamps line window ledges, doors are left open and **rangoli** patterns made of coloured powders and sands are outside the house.
- The next day is seen as a new beginning – debts have been paid, arguments settled, resolutions are made, husbands give their wives jewellery and wedding vows are renewed, children receive lots of presents and families share festive foods. Good has overcome evil and the New Year begins.

Diwali celebrations in the northern Indian city of Chandigarh.

The origins of Holi

Traditions tell of Prahlad, who was a prince. His father, the king, wanted all the people to worship him but the prince refused and worshipped **Vishnu** instead. Holika, the king's sister, tricked her nephew Prahlad into sitting on her lap in a bonfire in order to destroy him. Legend has it that she was immune to fire and would not burn. However, because she was misusing her powers for evil reasons, the plan went wrong – Prahlad walked out unharmed and Holika burnt in the flames.

Holi celebrations in Nandgaon, India.

In some areas of India, statues of Holika are burnt on fires (like Guy Fawkes on Bonfire Night). The ashes from the fire are seen to bring good luck.

Some Hindus believe that Holi is linked to Krishna. Hindus believe Krishna is the god Vishnu in human form. When Krishna was young he used to be very playful and threw coloured water over the milkmaids and this is what developed into the practical jokes and fun of Holi.

Holi is celebrated to mark the coming of spring so it is usually in March. Although it is a religious festival, it is also a time for fun.

- It is a really colourful festival with singing, dancing and people throwing coloured water and powders over each other.
- Families light bonfires, roast grains and throw popcorn and coconuts. Everyone, no matter what age, goes into the streets and joins in with the paint throwing.
- It is a time when everyone goes a little crazy and gets very excited. One purpose is to bring everyone together, including all religions. Children have great fun covering each other and in particular their parents with the coloured powder.

Activity C

Research a Hindu festival.

1 Find out about the symbolism of the festival.

2 Find out how different Hindus celebrate this festival, and try to explain why they celebrate it in different ways.

Kumbha Mela

The word 'Kumbha' means jug and 'Mela' means festival. So in effect **Kumbha Mela** means festival of the jug! This festival and **pilgrimage** is based on a legend and last took place in 2001.

The legend of Kumbha Mela

There is a legend about a battle between the gods and the demons (good and evil) over a jug which contained nectar. If someone drank it, it gave people immortality. This means that people would never die – they would live forever.

In the end the gods won but in winning four drops of the nectar were spilled at four sites. These sites are the bases for the festival, and it moves between them. There is a celebration every three years rotating around the four sites. Each twelfth-year celebration is known as Kumbha Mela. Which year is the next celebration?

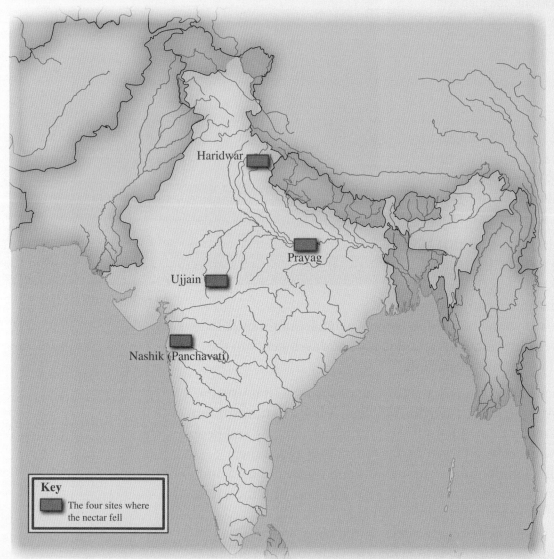

A map showing the four sites where the nectar fell.

32

The Kumbha Mela festival

At this festival in Prayag pilgrims (people who want to make a journey to a special place) meet at the place where the River Ganges, River Yamuna and River Sarasvah meet. Hindus believe the river washes away their sins. So they bathe in the holy river.

Once purified, the soul attains **moksha**, which means it can escape from the cycle of birth and death. Hindus also believe this river gives them purity, wealth and fertility.

Kumbha Mela is a festival and a pilgrimage. For many it is the most important thing they will do in their religious lives. In 2001 it was attended by more than 80 million people. That is more people than live in the UK.

Activity D

Imagine you are a reporter. You have been to Kumbha Mela and witnessed the celebrations. You have interviewed pilgrims who travelled from the UK for this festival. Write the script for your radio programme about the festival. You need to describe the scenes (remember radio is sound only), and include the interviews. Working in a group, record the programme for the class to listen to.

The **big** assignment

Task

To design a set of six stamps and to provide the material to explain your choice of designs.

Objectives

- To plan, design and colour a set of six stamps based on the topic areas covered.

- To provide reasons as to the choices you have made about your design and the symbolism to be found in your stamps.

Outcome

To produce a colourful and well designed set of six stamps, along with a detailed explanation of each stamp. Your teacher may give you a template to use or you can use your own design.

You could cover the following:

- the beginning of Hinduism

- the holy books

- the Ramayana

- the mandir

- Hindu rites of passage

- Hindu festivals and celebrations

- symbols associated with them

- meanings and celebrations.

Guidance

1   Hinduism is a very creative religion and many aspects of it are in picture form. The scriptures and temples are covered with teachings in picture form, especially in ancient times, so this is your chance to be creative.

2   Think about the topics you have covered so far and decide for yourself which parts you are going to include in your stamp collection.

3   If you are good at art, you can design by hand, but if not, don't worry: make use of ICT resources and search the Internet for images of temples, etc.

4   You might want to think about a colour scheme or a theme to run through your stamps.

5   You can use the template your teacher gives you or you can design your own way of presentation.

6   You need to write about your stamp – say what it is and give a little bit of information about it. For example, if you have used photographs, where were they taken? A temple in Britain or India maybe? Give your readers a little bit of education about Hinduism.

7   You need to explain why you chose these images and/or text. What were you hoping to show your readers?

8   Also your stamps will contain symbolism because pictures always do – what are the meanings of these images? For example, you might have a stamp with Rama and Sita and a lamp on it. Explain to your readers what that represents. This is the most difficult part of the assignment and takes you to a higher level of assessment.

9   Finally, you need to include some self-assessment – what do you think about your designs? Would you do anything different if you did them it again? Could they be better? What do you think are the good things about your designs?

Assessment

You will be assessed on:

✓ how well you have planned and presented your design

✓ how well you have explained your design and the choices you made

✓ your ability to explain the symbolism of your design and what it tells you about Hinduism.

Learning objectives

You will ...
- find out about the terms 'Brahman' and 'Ultimate Reality'
- understand the concept of God in Hinduism
- understand what the Trimurti is
- find out about the main characteristics of Brahma, Vishnu and Shiva.

The Ultimate Reality

Hindus believe in One Supreme God called **Brahman**. Brahman is thought to be everywhere and in everything. God is so great an idea that it is beyond our understanding. We can never see and understand fully. God has no limits so can be viewed in many ways. Some see God as a personality so they can build a relationship with God – like we do with each other. Yet God has superhuman-like qualities.

Therefore God is a difficult idea to explain. Hindus find it hard to answer the questions: What is God? Where is God? Why is God? How is God?

Nevertheless, if people are going to believe and worship, they have to have some idea or image to be able to do this. So Hindus break the idea of God down into what some believe to be about 33 million different parts called **deities**. Each deity is one of the functions of Brahman. It is like a different quality or characteristic. Each quality is represented as an image or a statue.

The **Trimurti** is the starting point of breaking Brahman down into ideas that human beings can understand. Trimurti means 'three forms', the three images of God: **Brahma**, **Vishnu** and **Shiva**.

Statues of the Trimurti in an UNESCO World Heritage Site, Elephanta Island, off Mumbai, India. The carving dates from between the ninth and eleventh centuries.

Hindus believe that God **creates** us all, **makes** all things so God is the **creator**. During their lives Hindus **ask God for help** in their lives so God is the **preserver**. God also **takes lives** so God is the **destroyer**.

Vishnu is blue like the sky to show he is everywhere. He has three lines on his forehead to show part of the Trimurti and four arms to show power.

He carries four objects showing the things he is responsible for. The conch shell represents the sound of creation. The discus symbolises the sun. The lotus flower is a symbol of peace and freedom. And the mace (club) is his magical weapon.

Vishnu is the preserver and protects our world. Vishnu came to earth in many forms (**avatars**) with special powers to help people.

Shiva is shown with a third eye, displaying the wisdom he has.

The cobra necklace shows Shiva's power over the most dangerous creatures. Also the snake shows Shiva's power of destruction and recreation. The snake sheds its skin to make way for new, smooth skin.

Brahma is the creator of the universe.

The three lines across his forehead in white ash represent Shiva's superhuman power and wealth. They cover up his powerful third eye.

Brahma is shown with four heads so that everything can be seen. Brahma has four arms (showing power), and carries a ladle with water, a string of beads (a reminder to pray) and a book (to represent the **Vedas**).

A three-pronged spear called a Trident represents the Trimurti.

Shiva is often seen dressed in animal skin, in cross-legged position. Parvati, his consort, is sometimes shown at the side of Shiva. She is usually represented as smiling and peaceful.

Vishnu is shown In two main ways: he is either standing on a lotus flower with **Lakshmi**, his consort, close by him or he is lying on the coils of a serpent, with Lakshmi massaging his feet.

Sometimes Vishnu is shown riding on Garuda, the King of Birds, who is half man, half eagle.

Shiva is the destroyer – which allows him to recreate. Shiva takes life, which is a positive thing because this allows new life. Shiva is often shown as a holy man meditating in deep thought. In some of his forms he is seen dancing in flames stamping on a demon.

Knowledge check

1 What is the name of God in Hinduism?
2 List three things about the Ultimate Reality.
3 What does 'Trimurti' mean?
4 Which three deities make up the Trimurti?
5 Explain why Hindus 'break God down' into parts.

Activity A

Imagine you have been asked to invent a superhero for a comic. The superhero should have powers and weapons that he or she can use to fight against evil.

1 What would your superhero be called? What would (s)he look like? What superpowers would (s)he have? What weapons would (s)he have?

2 Draw your superhero and write a paragraph to explain how (s)he could combat evil in the world.

Activity B

Draw a mural of the Trimurti so that anyone looking at it can understand what the Trimurti is and what their powers are.

Activity C

Find out more about the Trimurti. Write an essay to explain which of the Trimurti is most important and why.

Activity D

'Hindus believe in many different gods.'

What reasons might someone have for saying this? What do you think about the statement? How might someone argue against it?

2.2 What do Hindus believe about deities?

Learning objectives

You will ...
- identify and learn about some well known Hindu deities
- understand the symbolism and meanings in the images of Hindu deities
- assess why Hindus choose to worship certain gods/goddesses and evaluate their importance for Hindu society.

In Hinduism, deities can be either gods or goddesses. The images often have superhuman elements to them to remind Hindus that the images are not what God actually looks like but to symbolise the power, wisdom and qualities of God. Look at the selection of images below and on page 40 (and the picture of the Trimurti on page 37) and see if you can spot the superhuman aspects.

Look at the selection of images below and on page 40 (and the picture of the Trimurti on page 37)

Lakshmi

Lakshmi is the companion of the god Vishnu. She is one of the most popular goddesses of Hindu mythology and is known as the goddess of happiness, wealth, purity and good fortune.

Lakshmi is sometimes shown as a beautiful woman with four arms, standing on a lotus flower and holding lotus flowers in her hands.

She is always pictured close to Vishnu, and often seated on the coils of a serpent, massaging Vishnu's feet. She may be dressed in a red sari. The colour red symbolises prosperity.

She is sometimes seen giving blessings to people and offering gold coins to those who worship her. Good luck is attached to her.

She may have elephants behind her, anointing her with water. Elephants symbolise good fortune.

Knowledge check

Look at all the deities on pages 39–41.

1. What qualities does Lakshmi represent?
2. Whose companion is she?
3. Which is the most popular deity?
4. Which instrument does Krishna play?
5. Whose wife is Parvati?
6. Ganesha's head comes from which animal?

Krishna

Krishna is possibly the most popular deity. He has two hands playing a flute which is said to make worshippers feel love towards God.

He wears a yellow/orange robe and has a peacock feather in his hair.

His skin colour is blue/black like a rain cloud.

He often has cows behind him. He is always seen as youthful even though he is thought to have lived to 125 years. God does not die so Krishna does not age.

Krishna is often shown with his companion Radha – the love that they share is not physical but a spiritual love that brings people to God.

The gods and goddesses in Hinduism have many myths and legends written about them. Remember the **Smriti**? (See Chapter 1.2, pages 6–9.) Smriti are about the gods. It is much easier to pass on ideas in the form of stories because they are easily remembered. Most of these are **epic** (long) stories about when the deities came to earth in many different forms. There is usually a battle between good and evil at the centre of them.

The stories are really important at **festival** time, as most festivals are based around them. Hindu children love the stories, and learn about their religion through them.

How Ganesha got his head

The story of the birth of **Ganesha** goes like this …

One day, the goddess Parvati was bathing. She created a boy out of the dirt and gave him the task of guarding the entrance to her room.

When her husband Shiva returned, he was surprised to find a stranger stopping him from going in to his room. He struck off the boy's head in rage. Parvati broke down in grief. Out of compassion, Shiva sent out his squad to fetch the head of any sleeping being that was facing the north. They found a sleeping elephant and brought back its severed head. This was attached to the body of the boy. Shiva brought the boy back to life and made him the leader of his troops.

Activity A

1 Write a quiz to test people's knowledge of Hindu deities.

2 Include multiple-choice answers in your quiz, i.e. a choice of four, one of which is correct.

How Ganesha lost his tusk

There are several stories which tell us how Ganesha lost his tusk. One of those stories talks of how Parashurama fought with Ganesha. Parashurama was travelling around the world killing wicked kings. He had been given a special axe to do this task after he had prayed to Shiva. He wanted to show Shiva he was very grateful, and so went to Mount Kailash. Ganesha was guarding Shiva's palace there, and wouldn't let Parashurama pass. He said Shiva had to give permission, so Parashurama had to wait. Parashurama believed he was such a devoted follower, he shouldn't need to wait, so he lost his temper. He fought with Ganesha, and broke his tusk. Shiva then appeared and told Parashurama off, who then begged forgiveness from Ganesha. And so, Ganesha was left with only one tusk.

The story of Narasimha

As **Narasimha**, Vishnu comes in the form of half-man, half-lion.

The king of demons wanted to remain young and never die. To this end, he meditated to Brahma. The gods were frightened of the king of demons and asked Brahma to quieten him. Brahma was impressed by the king's meditation and granted him a wish. The king wished that he be killed by neither man nor beast, neither in daylight nor at night, neither inside nor outside a building.

With his wish being granted, the king believed himself to be the supreme God. He banned all worship of gods by anyone – but his son, Prahlad, worshipped Vishnu. This enraged the king very much. He ordered many ways to kill Prahlad, including asking his sister Holika to sit with Prahlad in the fire. You can read that story (and the origins of **Holi**) in more detail on page 31.

But Prahlad escaped unhurt every time. Angrily the king asked Prahlad to show him Vishnu. Prahlad said, 'He is everywhere'. Further enraged, the king knocked down a pillar, and asked if Vishnu was present there.

Vishnu, as Narasimha, then leapt from the pillar. He was neither man, nor beast. The pillar was neither inside the house nor outside, and the time was evening, neither night nor day. He killed the king and saved the life of his devotee, Prahlad.

Activity B

1 Write a story about good overcoming evil.

2 Explain what the moral of your story is. What can people learn from it?

Activity C

1 Compile a directory of symbols used in illustrations of Hindu deities.

2 Describe each of the symbols and find a picture of it. Then explain what it represents to Hindu believers.

Activity D

1 Explain how each of the Hindu deities may have powers that could help people living in modern Britain.

2 For each deity, explain what problems they may help with.

Learning objectives

You will ...
- find out about the concepts of samsara and moksha
- understand Hinduism in the form of a continuous cycle of life
- look at the issue of life after death.

Samsara

'As the soul continuously passes, in this body, from birth to youth to old age, the soul similarly passes into another body at death. A self-realised soul is not bewildered by such a change.'

(Bhagavad Gita, Chapter 2)

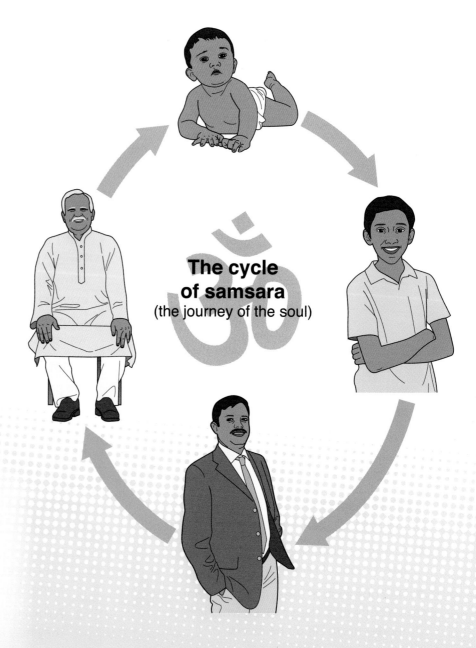

The cycle of samsara (the journey of the soul)

What happens when we die is one of life's most difficult questions. What do you think? Why do you think this? Is death the start or the end? Do we go to heaven/paradise or hell? Do we come back to this life? Or is death simply it ... the end?

Hindus believe that life does not begin at birth and end at death. Rather it flows from birth, through life, to death, and to rebirth of the **soul** (Hindus call it the **atman**). The soul is the part of us which is not physical – our inner self or spirit. Hindus believe it is reborn many times. The word **samsara** means 'to flow', and is used to refer to the continuous flow or cycle of life.

The soul takes a new form to continue to exist. The soul that moves on takes with it the character it has built up. So how we behave and what we have learnt about in life now, goes with the soul for a next life. This means that Hindus create their next rebirth. This is known as the law of **karma**, where there are consequences for all actions. Karma is the belief that good actions have good consequences, and bad actions have bad consequences. However, we need to recognise that life is more complicated than this, and lots of factors influence the decisions we make. The word 'karma' means action. The consequences often come in the next lifetime(s).

Hindus believe that their souls keep being reborn until they are ready to end the cycle of rebirth. Then they search for a way out to end the cycle. There is no god who judges Hindus at death so there is no idea of heaven and hell.

In Hinduism the aim is to achieve **moksha** – no longer to be reborn. Hindus believe that when their souls become enlightened, they escape from the cycle of rebirth, achieving moksha. Being enlightened is knowing the truth about everything, being free of cares and desires. Hindus can do this in several ways, including religious study, through helping others, through meditation, and through devotion to God.

Knowledge check

1 What is a soul?

2 What is the law of karma?

3 What is moksha?

Activity A

Look at the quotation from the Bhagavad Gita on page 42.

1 What do you think it is trying to say? Write down what you think.

2 Discuss your answers together as a class.

Activity B

1 What do you believe happens when you die? Discuss your answers together as a class.

2 How many different ideas are there? Could you all agree on the same thing?

3 What does the diagram on page 42 tell you about what Hindus think?

Activity C

Create your own moksha 'Game of Life':

1 This should be a snakes and ladders board. On the squares with the snake's head there should be an action written which the player thinks would lead to a person not achieving moksha.

2 On the squares with the bottom of the ladders on them there should be an action written which could be seen to help someone achieve moksha.

3 Play the game.

Activity D

'Life cannot stop altogether at death.'

1 What do you think about this statement?

2 In your answer, show that you have thought about Hindu ideas of reincarnation and other views on life after death.

3 Show also that you have thought about Hindu ideas about atman (see pages 44–45).

2.4 What do Hindus believe about karma?

Learning objectives

You will ...
- find out about the Hindu idea of reincarnation (life after death)
- understand how the caste system works
- understand the concept of karma
- compare the idea of reincarnation with other ideas of life after death.

Hindus believe that the soul (the atman) lives forever. When a person dies the atman is reborn into another form and this depends upon karma – the idea that all our actions in life have consequences and these consequences affect our rebirth. Every living thing has a connection with God and it takes many lifetimes before the soul is enlightened enough to attain moksha and not be reborn.

The caste system and reincarnation

In India, a **caste** is a level of society a person is born into. Some are born into a caste of privilege, and some are born into very humble circumstances. The caste into which a person is born tends to be fixed for their lifetime, and people from different castes tend not to mix with each other.

Hindus believe that the caste a person is born into is decided by their karma. This means that their actions from a previous life determine the circumstances they will be born into. The idea that a soul can be born into a new body to live another lifetime is called **reincarnation**.

Brahmins (priests)

Kshatriyas (soldiers and rulers)

Vaishyas (shopkeepers, farmers and skilled workers)

Shudras (unskilled workers)

Dalits/Untouchables

The five castes.

As you can see in the diagram on page 44, Indian society is split into five groups: four **varnas** (castes or classes) and a lower group of people called the 'Dalits'. Dalit means 'downtrodden', and Dalits are sometimes known as 'Untouchables'. The higher up the system you are, the nearer to God you are and therefore nearer to the escape from another rebirth. So, if a person is born in the human state as a Shudra, for example, this means that the soul still has many lifetimes to go here on earth before it is freed from rebirth.

Today the system is not as rigid. For example, there are occasions where people can work their way out of poverty, and there is a chance of an education for people born into unskilled families, which could help them improve themselves.

Many Hindus today, especially Western Hindus, believe the caste system to be wrong.

Knowledge check

1 What is the atman?

2 What is the caste system?

3 What are the five varnas?

4 How has the system changed in India today?

Activity A

Make a wall display to explain karma.

1 On one side, show the kinds of jobs and activities a person might do to create good karma.

2 On the other side, show the jobs and activities that would lead to bad karma.

Activity C

Write a story about 'A day in the life of …'. The things that happen to the character in the story must by the end of the day balance the karma of the person – so include good actions/decisions and bad actions/decisions.

The Hindu idea of karma

Hindus believe that in their lives people have free choices about what they do and so the decisions they make will either add to their good karma or create bad karma.

There are also lower states than the human ones. This is how it works:

• First, souls which are not human (animals and other life forms) do not gain good karma because animals act on instinct, not by making moral decisions. So all they are doing during these lifetimes is burning off the bad karma from previous lifetimes.

• Humans can drop out of the human state if their actions are so bad.

• Good karma can only be created in human lifetimes.

• When a soul dies it waits for its rebirth. If it is going to be a good rebirth, it is a bit like the soul having a holiday before it returns. If it is a bad rebirth, it is a bit like the soul knows it is waiting to go to prison.

Activity B

The caste system used to dictate how you would earn a living: you would be trained to do the work your father did.

1 Can you think of any advantages to this system?

2 Can you think of the disadvantages?

Activity D

1 Compare the different ideas about life after death:

• one lifetime with heaven or hell at the end of it
• the idea of Hindu rebirth.

2 Look at the advantages/disadvantages of each. Which idea do you prefer?

3 Find out about the life of Dr B. R. Ambedkar, and what he did to fight against Untouchability.

2.5 What do Hindus believe about creation and science?

Learning objectives

You will ...
- find out about two creation myths
- research a Hindu creation myth
- understand the ideas behind the creation myths
- explore creation ideas in Hinduism and those suggested by science.

According to some mythological texts, there are many universes, like bubbles in space. In this universe there are three regions:

the **heavenly planets**, the **earthly realm** and the **lower regions**.

Hindu creation stories

> 'But, after all, who knows, and who can say, when it was born and how creation happened?
> The gods are later than the world's creation. Who knows then when creation truly began?'
> (Rig Veda)

The sacrifice of Purusha

In this creation story, Hindus say that the universe came from **Purusha**, the cosmic giant.

Purusha was sacrificed by the gods. He was split into pieces and from these pieces, the world came into existence.

The sun and the moon, the universe and all life came from Purusha. The heavens came from his head, the earth from his feet and the sky from his ear. The universe itself came from his navel.

Purusha also created the four castes in life: the Brahmins (priests) came from his mouth, the Kshatriyas (rulers) came from his arms, the Vaishyas (shopkeepers, traders and farmers) from his thighs and the Shudras (unskilled workers) from his feet.

Vishnu and the creation of the world – a story from mythology

If you could go back in time, before time and the universe even existed, you would see nothing. There *was* nothing. There was an empty blackness which stretched as far as it was possible to see.

The blackness seemed to sway like an ocean. If you could have seen it, you would have noticed that floating on the blackness was a cobra. This cobra was huge, seemingly endless in its length.

Lying on the cobra, fast asleep, was the Lord Vishnu. The cobra watched over him, and kept him safe, making sure his dreams would be undisturbed.

All at once, a humming sound began, which got louder and louder. It stirred Vishnu from his sleep. The dawn began to break and the blackness receded. From Vishnu's navel, a lotus flower began to grow, and when it opened, it revealed Brahma.

Vishnu turned to Brahma and commanded him to begin the creation. Brahma bowed to his master, and began his work. Suddenly, a wind began to blow. The sea and the cobra (with Vishnu) vanished. All that remained was Brahma in his lotus flower.

The endless sea threw him about angrily. Brahma raised his arms and calmed the waves. He tore the lotus into three parts, and from the three parts made the heavens, the earth and the sky.

Brahma then began to create the details on the earth because it was empty. He covered the earth with plants and trees. Then he created the animals, insects and birds. He gave them the five senses. The earth was colourful, noisy and full of life.

So what do we know about Hindu ideas about creation?

It doesn't really matter whether these creation stories are true or not; or even if they have only a bit of truth in them. They were written by people who didn't have all the scientific knowledge we have nowadays. They had to try to work out from what they could see an answer to the question of where the universe and humans all came from. If all you had was what you could see, you might not come up with anything very different.

Hindus believe that:

> This is not the first universe: countless universes have existed before this one.

> The universe, like the life forms that exist within it, is born, lives, and is destroyed, to be born again.

> God is responsible for the creation, maintenance and destruction of the universe.

> All life comes from God.

Hinduism and science

Some people claim that the ancient Hindu stories about the creation of the universe agree with modern scientific theories.

- Ancient Hindu theories suggest that the universe was created many billions of years ago. Modern scientists believe it started about 13.6 billion years ago.
- Hinduism teaches that, before the universe was created, there was nothing – no space and no time. Scientists agree.
- Hindu creation stories from Hindu mythology say that the universe started as a single, round object, like an egg. Scientists today believe that the universe began as a 'singularity': a ball of immense mass.
- The Hindu stories describe the universe getting bigger and bigger as it develops. Science teaches that the universe is expanding.
- Hindus believe that there are many universes. So do some scientists.
- Hinduism teaches that the universe will one day shrink back into nothing and the process of creation will start again. Some modern scientists also believe this.

What do you think about the Big Bang theory?

Knowledge check

1 Who was Purusha?
2 How did Brahma create the world according to mythology?
3 What are the important messages from the creation stories?

Activity A

Write a quiz to test your classmate's memory about the story of how the universe was created.

Activity B

Use the Internet to find out about the scientific theory of the Big Bang. Draw a timeline of it.

Activity C

Research Hindu creation stories.

1 Can you find a different story or a different version of one of the stories you have read so far? Write about what you find from your research.
2 Why do you think that there are different creation stories? Try to come up with at least three reasons.

Activity D

The American astronomer, Carl Sagan, said: 'Hinduism is the only religion whose time-scale for the universe matches the billions of years documented by modern science.'

Use the information in this chapter and your own research to make a PowerPoint presentation showing areas where modern science and Hinduism agree about the creation of the universe.

2.6 What happens at a Hindu funeral?

Learning objectives

You will ...
- find out what happens at a Hindu funeral
- compare Hindu funerals in India and in Britain
- understand how religious practices can be influenced by culture.

We have already seen that the birth ceremonies and **Sacred Thread Ceremonies** are carried out following teachings from the scriptures. The scriptures also set down how funerals should be carried out:

- Hindus are cremated rather than buried (although young babies/children are not).
- The body is bathed and dressed in a clean white cloth, placed on a stretcher made of bamboo and carried to the cremation area.
- In India this would be near a river like the Ganges.
- A male relative (usually the son) walks in front carrying a pot of coals. Slow-burning logs are used to build a pyre. Sometimes some sandalwood can be used as it smells sweet.
- The body is placed on the pyre with the head pointing north.
- The eldest son walks three times around the pyre and uses a burning stick to light the fire at the four corners.
- When burning starts, five spoonfuls of ghee are offered to Agni (the Hindu god of fire) and incense is put into the flames. The priest leads the prayers.
- Hindus believe that when the skull cracks the soul is released. Walking around it prevents the soul coming straight back to earth as a ghost, which would haunt the living.
- When the fire is cooled the ashes are collected and scattered into the water or the river.

A funeral pyre on the River Ganges.

Knowledge check

1 Which three ceremonies have God and the scriptures at the centre of them?

2 What happens to the body before it is cremated?

3 How is it taken to the place of cremation?

4 Explain what happens at the funeral pyre.

Activity A

Write an interview with the son of a Hindu family whose elderly mother has passed away. Your interviewee should describe what happens at a Hindu funeral and some of the son's beliefs about life after death.

What happens in Britain?

In Britain cremations cannot take place in the same way as in India. Cremations are not allowed to take place in the open air. Some Hindus actually take the body of a relative back to India so that they can be disposed of correctly.

In Britain a coffin is used, rather than wrapping the body in cloth. Local crematoriums try to follow the traditional Hindu funeral rites as closely as British law allows. For example, the coffin can be walked around, incense sticks burnt and teachings read.

A Hindu memorial service in the UK.

In Britain, instead of scattering the ashes in a local river, there are memorials for Hindus as special places to remember the dead. Look at the photo above showing a Hindu memorial in Britain. Notice how traditional Hindu and British cultures come together in the surroundings and the light effect.

The first open-air cremation took place in the UK in July 2006, in Northumberland. Newcastle City Council said the burning of human remains anywhere outside a crematorium was prohibited.

In February 2010, a Hindu man, Davender Ghai, won the right to be cremated on a traditional funeral pyre. Judges decided it was lawful after Mr Ghai said it could include walls and a roof with an opening.

Activity B

Imagine that there will be a range of visitors present at a Hindu funeral. Use the details above to design an order of events for the funeral service which will be helpful for them to understand what is happening and why. Research or draw your own images.

Activity C

Explain how and why Hindu funerals in Britain are different from those conducted in India.

Activity D

'Hindus in the UK should be allowed to conduct funerals as they are conducted in India.'

1 What do you think? Should people have the right to practise their religion without interference from the law?

2 Try to present arguments for and against the statement.

The big assignment

Task

To design a set of magazine articles on Hindu beliefs studied in this section.

Objectives

- To plan, design and colour a set of articles for a magazine for young people.
- To provide information so that readers can learn about Hindu beliefs in an interesting way.

Outcome

To produce a magazine about Hindu beliefs. It should be aimed at a readership age of ten to fourteen.

You should include information about:

- Hindu beliefs about God – the Ultimate Reality
- the Trimurti – Brahma, Vishnu and Shiva
- the deities
- samsara and moksha
- the law of karma
- reincarnation
- funerals.

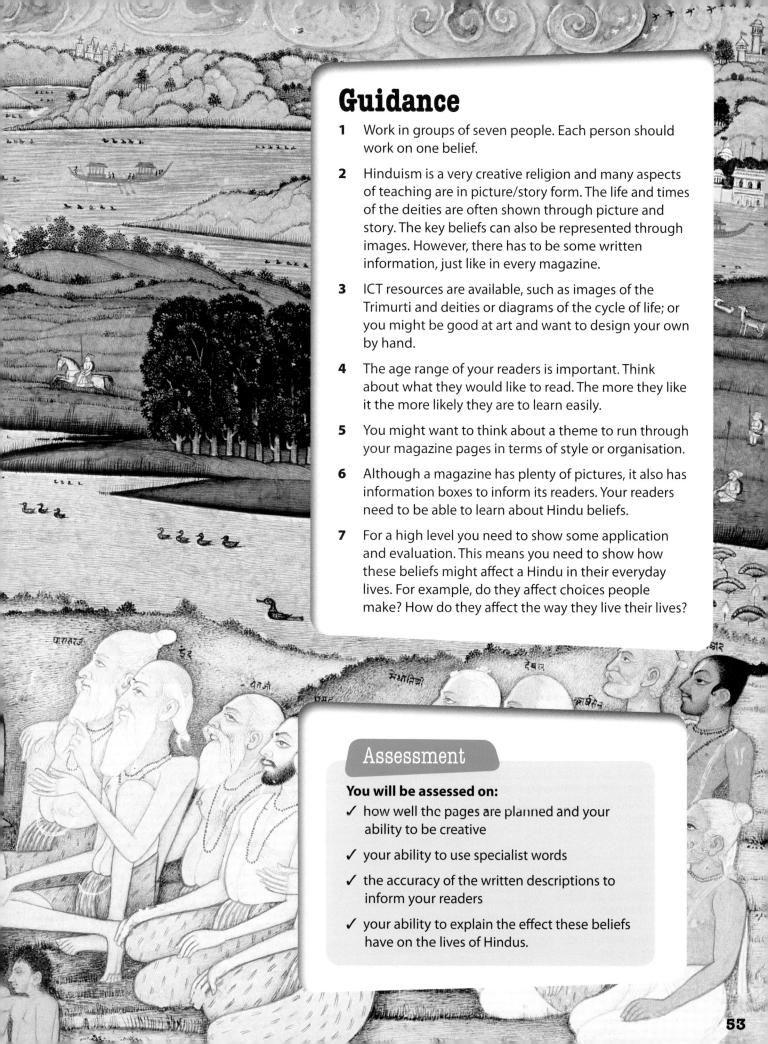

Guidance

1   Work in groups of seven people. Each person should work on one belief.

2   Hinduism is a very creative religion and many aspects of teaching are in picture/story form. The life and times of the deities are often shown through picture and story. The key beliefs can also be represented through images. However, there has to be some written information, just like in every magazine.

3   ICT resources are available, such as images of the Trimurti and deities or diagrams of the cycle of life; or you might be good at art and want to design your own by hand.

4   The age range of your readers is important. Think about what they would like to read. The more they like it the more likely they are to learn easily.

5   You might want to think about a theme to run through your magazine pages in terms of style or organisation.

6   Although a magazine has plenty of pictures, it also has information boxes to inform its readers. Your readers need to be able to learn about Hindu beliefs.

7   For a high level you need to show some application and evaluation. This means you need to show how these beliefs might affect a Hindu in their everyday lives. For example, do they affect choices people make? How do they affect the way they live their lives?

Assessment

You will be assessed on:

✓ how well the pages are planned and your ability to be creative

✓ your ability to use specialist words

✓ the accuracy of the written descriptions to inform your readers

✓ your ability to explain the effect these beliefs have on the lives of Hindus.

3.1 How do Hindus make moral decisions?

Learning objectives

You will ... • find out about what a moral issue is
• understand how people make moral decisions
• evaluate the ideas of right and wrong.

Hindus use the word dharma to mean the beliefs, teachings, actions and behaviours that keep the world running smoothly. It refers to the **duty** a person has to do the right thing.

If you believe something, then it influences your decisions and your actions. In Hinduism, there are some key beliefs and teachings that affect the ways that Hindus make decisions. Put them all together, and you have a jigsaw for moral behaviour: dharma. Let's have a look at some of the pieces.

Hindus can follow the examples set by the deities in some of the stories built up around them, and by seeking guidance from Hindu teachers.

Hindus believe that all of our thoughts, words and actions generate positive and negative energies. This **karma** builds up to shape our next lifetime (lots of positive actions mean a good life, whereas lots of negative actions mean the opposite). Harming other beings creates bad karma.

Dharmasastras are Hindu texts that provide guidance on putting the dharma into practice. They provide teachings on how to live properly in the world.

To create good karma, it is not enough just to do good: a person should try to be good. This means that, when you do a good deed, you should do it from a real desire to make life better.

Hindus believe that prayer helps make wise decisions.

Because all beings are interlinked and are part of God, Hinduism teaches ahimsa (non-violence) – the idea that harming any form of life harms life itself.

Hindus believe that everything is interlinked and interdependent.

Hindus believe all life is sacred – human, animal and plant. All are created from God, and each is part of God.

Souls seek **moksha** – an end to rebirth and spiritual union with God. The creation of good karma leads a soul to moksha.

Hindus are prepared to learn from the wisdom of their elders and put their advice into action.

Mahatma Gandhi was an Indian leader during the time Indians were trying to free themselves from British rule. He taught ahimsa to his followers. He said, 'There are many causes that I am prepared to die for, but no causes that I am prepared to kill for.'

This cartoon from *Punch*, 1932, shows Gandhi fasting in protest against the segregation of India's 'Untouchables'.

Knowledge check

1 What is dharma?
2 Why should people try to create good karma?
3 What is ahimsa?
4 What are dharmasastras?

Activity A

Using information from this chapter, make a booklet to help young Hindus know which ideas they should consider when making moral decisions.

Activity B

Look back at some of the stories about Hindu deities and the lessons that can be learned from them. Use them to draw up a list of rules and guidance that might help Hindus when they have to make moral decisions.

Activity C

Do you agree with the idea of ahimsa? Find out more about it before you give your response.

Activity D

1 What are the most important causes in the world today that you feel strongly about?
2 Do you agree with Gandhi's view on ahimsa? Find out more about his life and teachings to help you frame your response.

Learning objectives

You will ...
- find out about Hindu attitudes to marriage
- find out about Hindu attitudes to sexual relationships
- explore Hindu attitudes to family life.

In Hinduism, marriage is very important. Marriage is one of the sixteen **samskaras**. It is recommended that every Hindu should marry and have children as part of their religion (with the exception of holy men). There are ideals about who Hindus should marry, and how they should live.

Arranged marriages

Most Hindus marry the person their parents agree for them to marry. This is called an arranged marriage. Parents find a person who is compatible and considered to be the best match for their child.

Meetings will be arranged for the two people to get to know their potential partner a little, and they can then decide for themselves whether they wish to marry. Often a priest will have been consulted to cast horoscopes for the couple to show they are a good match.

In a way the two families are joining through this marriage – it is much more than just the couple involved. The partner should be of the same **caste** and of the same religion. This way, any children will be brought up in the Hindu faith.

Hindu attitudes to sexual relationships

For a Hindu man, his life is split into four ashramas (stages). The second stage is that of a family man, or grihastha (householder), and it is only in this stage that he should have any sexual relationships.

Sex is seen as a gift from the Ultimate Reality (God) and is to produce children as well as for enjoyment. Any sex outside marriage is considered unacceptable. To have sex before marriage would be to go against the rules of purity and cleanliness. Adultery (having an affair) also causes harm to your partner, so is a kind of ahimsa.

Hinduism stresses the need for a son to carry out certain religious rituals, and so sons are highly prized. This has led to bigger families, as well as a problem with female infanticide and high numbers of abortions of female foetuses in India. This is not part of actual Hindu teaching.

Knowledge check

1 In which ashrama is it acceptable for a Hindu to have sexual relationships?

2 What is arranged marriage?

3 Why do Hindu couples try to have a son when they marry?

Activity A

1 Write a test with five questions on this topic.

2 Give it to someone to complete in your class.

Activity B

Find out about traditional Hindu wedding ceremonies. Design a card inviting a non-Hindu to a Hindu wedding. Include information that will help your guest understand about marriage in Hinduism.

Activity C

Imagine you have set up a company to help Hindus find a suitable partner for marriage. Design a questionnaire which Hindus can fill in to have their details processed and to use your service.

Activity D

Think about arranged marriage in Hinduism. It has been said that in Hinduism, a couple's relationship begins cool and grows hot through the process of an arranged marriage.

1 Give reasons for and against arranged marriage – you must come up with at least three of each.

2 Use your reasoning to hold a debate with others in your class.

3.3 What does Hinduism teach about prejudice?

Learning objectives

You will ... • find out what prejudice and discrimination mean

• understand Hindu attitudes to race, religious prejudice and sexuality.

People who are prejudiced, prejudge others. They have an idea about them before they get to know them and base their opinions on that. It can affect the way they treat them or behave towards them – those actions are what we call discrimination.

It is common to find prejudice and discrimination in society, but in some forms it can be very destructive to people's lives. We are going to look at two kinds of discrimination.

The flag and symbol for the Arya Samaj. In the centre is the Aum sign, considered by them to be the highest and most proper name of God. They do not believe in the hereditary caste system.

Racial prejudice

Race has always been an issue in India. The castes are known as '**varnas**' which actually means 'colour'. Hindu scriptures talk about dividing people into groups, so many Hindus still follow the caste system. People were separated into groups related to their colour of skin – the darker the skin, the lower the caste. The lower castes were often treated badly and groups did not intermix.

Over the last few years things have changed, especially in big cities, but in Indian villages it is still rare for people to marry outside their caste and discrimination is common, even though it is illegal.

Hinduism has campaigned for the lowest castes to be treated better. The Indian leader Mahatma Gandhi, then the Arya Samaj (a Hindu reform movement) worked to change attitudes, and has had success in the cities of India.

Knowledge check

1 What is prejudice?

2 What is discrimination?

3 What is racial prejudice?

4 What is homophobia?

Activity A

Find out about Dayananda Saraswati, the founder of the Arya Samaj. Write a paragraph describing what he thought about the caste system. Try to add a quotation from him.

Sexuality

Prejudice against homosexuals is called **homophobia**. It exists in most societies. In many cultures and societies it is considered unacceptable, and there are laws to protect gay people from discrimination. Things are changing all over the world but the change is very slow.

It is very difficult for homosexuals in most of India. Gay Hindus in the UK are protected by law, but that doesn't mean they don't face prejudice and discrimination. Many gay people – Hindu or not – find that their own families disown them and cut them off.

In India, especially in the countryside, homosexuals often face much discrimination. People can be arrested and imprisoned. There have been many cases of Hindus being assaulted or murdered because they are gay. Until 2009, it was a criminal offence to be gay. However the UK Hindu Council said: 'Homosexual nature is part of the natural law of God; it should be accepted for what it is, no more and no less.'

I have always been taught that as a Hindu I am expected to go through the marriage stage and produce children, especially a son. This is one of the four ashramas (stages) of my life.

In Hindu scriptures there are texts that talk about the gods which hint that some had homosexual relationships, so for me being gay is acceptable. Most Hindus believe that some people are born gay – they are the creation of God and their way of being is natural, not wrong. Hindu tradition teaches that the sex of a child comes from the elements fire and water. If the fire is strongest the child is a boy and if the water is strongest it is a girl. If both are balanced then the child is homosexual. However, I know some still believe that a sexual relationship between two people of the same sex is wrong.

Activity B

Find out about Hindu attitudes to women. You could present your findings on a poster.

Activity C

Research the work of Gandhi, in particular his attitude to the Dalits 'Untouchables'. Analyse what he did and why he did it. Can you work out his motives in getting society to accept more fully this group of people?

Activity D

'It is acceptable to be sexist in some situations.'

1 Write down reasons to agree and disagree with this statement, using examples to illustrate your meaning.

2 Do you agree with that statement? Explain and justify your own viewpoint.

Learning objectives

You will ... • learn about the issues surrounding poverty, the environment and animal rights

• understand and analyse Hindu attitudes to poverty, the environment and animal rights.

Poverty

Poverty is when people do not have access to the basic needs of life – food, water, shelter, health care, education and employment. India is a very poor country where one-third of the world's poor live. Thirty-five per cent of people cannot read or write, 20 million children do not go to school and 1600 children die every day from drinking dirty water.

Although India is a very religious country there is a massive gap between the rich and poor. We have all heard of the millions spent in Bollywood and in Indian cricket, yet people live in terrible slums and children search for food on rubbish dumps and work in factories in very unsafe conditions for virtually nothing.

Sewa is selfless service to all life. Hindus believe that service towards others brings karmic benefit and enables a person to make progress to moksha. They also believe that sewa is service to God, since God is life.

Hindus must do sewa out of compassion and sympathy for the suffering of others. The diagram below shows what Hinduism teaches about poverty.

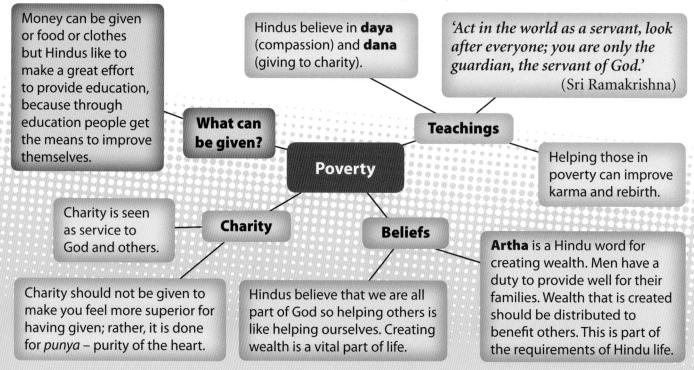

Money can be given or food or clothes but Hindus like to make a great effort to provide education, because through education people get the means to improve themselves.

Hindus believe in **daya** (compassion) and **dana** (giving to charity).

'*Act in the world as a servant, look after everyone; you are only the guardian, the servant of God.*' (Sri Ramakrishna)

What can be given?

Teachings

Poverty

Helping those in poverty can improve karma and rebirth.

Charity is seen as service to God and others.

Charity

Beliefs

Artha is a Hindu word for creating wealth. Men have a duty to provide well for their families. Wealth that is created should be distributed to benefit others. This is part of the requirements of Hindu life.

Charity should not be given to make you feel more superior for having given; rather, it is done for *punya* – purity of the heart.

Hindus believe that we are all part of God so helping others is like helping ourselves. Creating wealth is a vital part of life.

The environment

Hindus believe trees have an **atman** (soul), just like other living things. They are treated with respect because they are the most important type of plant. **Krishna** compares everything with the banyan tree because it is large and provides a home for many different creatures.

Humans and the environment have a close relationship. Pollution and global warming are major issues; we are responsible for this damage. Although human beings are seen as the most intelligent life form on earth, we are responsible for almost all the damage done to the planet.

Karma teaches that resources in the world become scarce because people waste them. People should not be selfish and should try not to damage the world. By doing this, they are repaying God for the gifts he has given.

The content of the Atharva Veda

Hindus are active in trying to focus on the future and what can be done to prevent further damage. They use teachings in the Atharva Veda to help them with this. The following are two examples of where teachings have formed the basis of Hindu action:

1   Hindus helped form the **Assisi Declarations**. One of the five Hindu statements is: *'Nature cannot be destroyed without humanity destroying itself.'*
2   The Bhumi Project is an organisation working to benefit the planet by creating green Hindu programmes for action. This includes green **pilgrimage**, Hindu labelling schemes, green **festivals** and gatherings and education.

> 'If there is but one tree of flowers and fruit within a village, that place is worthy of your respect.'
> (Mahabharata)

> 'The universe and every object in it has been created as an abode of the Supreme God meant for the benefit of all.'
> (Mahabharata)

> 'All kinds of remedies for human diseases are provided by the plants and trees of the earth.'
> (Varaha Purana)

> 'Trees have five sorts of kindness which are their daily sacrifice. To families they give fuel; to passersby they give shade and a resting place; to birds they give shelter; with their leaves, roots and bark they give medicines.'
> (Varaha Purana)

The banyan tree has religious significance for Hindus because of its longevity. This banyan tree in Dibrugarh, India has been turned into a **shrine**.

Animal rights

Hinduism has many general teachings about animals. In simple terms they should be treated well as they have feelings and their souls are reincarnated.

- Most Hindus are vegetarian.
- No Hindu will eat beef because cows are sacred to Hindus.
- Butchery and related jobs are restricted to people of low caste.
- Most Hindus believe human beings are superior to animals.
- Some Hindu gods have animal characteristics: **Ganesha** has the head of an elephant; **Hanuman** takes the form of a monkey. This emphasises that they treat animals with great respect.

Many of the Hindu gods have animals as servants, helpers and protectors. Here is **Shiva** with Nandi the bull. And Krishna had a cow. Can you find out more about these stories?

Cows

'Surely one who kills a cow or a bull commits a terrible crime.'
(Mahabharata)

The cow is regarded as sacred by Hindus. In Indian society cows have total freedom – it is common to see them in town centres, at the side of rivers just lazing and grazing. The cow provides food and drink (milk and butter), dung for fuel and for building bricks (shelter) and employment – in the fields they pull carts and plough the land, help with the harvests and carry things to markets.

Knowledge check

Look at pages 60–63.

1 What is poverty?

2 What is sewa?

3 Why do Hindus say we should look after the environment?

4 Why are the cow and the elephant special?

Elephants

Elephants are also highly regarded in Hindu culture. As the god Ganesha has elephant features, elephants can be found in large temples in the south of India. They can be seen in religious processions on major holy days but more often they are found in the temple grounds, giving blessings to the pilgrims who visit.

The pilgrim offers the elephant a banana or a rupee coin which the elephant takes with the end of its trunk and places the donation in its mouth or in its keeper's hands, as the case may be. Then the elephant taps (or knocks) the pilgrim on the head as a blessing.

Endangered animals

India is home to tigers and leopards, yet they have been hunted almost out of existence. Hindus have been at the forefront of wildlife programmes to protect India's animals.

One such project is the ambitious conservation effort named Project Tiger. Its aim is to increase the tiger population. A number of forest areas were declared national parks and funds allotted for protecting the tigers.

An Indian temple elephant.

Activity A

1 Make an information sheet for each of the three aspects of this topic – poverty, environment and animals.

2 For each, state what the problems are and what Hinduism teaches about it.

Activity B

Select one of the three aspects of this topic. Summarise Hindu attitudes to this. Provide examples of how a Hindu could live in such a way as to live up to these attitudes.

Activity C

1 Find out more about Hindu beliefs and teachings on the environment on the Alliance of Religions and Conservation website (**www.arcworld.org**). You will also find out about environmental projects undertaken by Hindu groups.

2 Use the results of your research to produce a booklet on Hinduism and environment showing how Hindu teachings affect work in the environment.

Activity D

'Poverty, environment, and animal welfare – none are more important than humans.'

1 Evaluate this statement to show whether Hindus agree or disagree.

2 What do you think? Do you agree or disagree with the statement?

Learning objectives

You will …
- find out what Hinduism teaches about the sanctity of life
- understand issues surrounding abortion and euthanasia
- be able to analyse Hindu teachings and beliefs about life and death issues.

Abortion

This is an operation which deliberately removes a foetus from a woman's womb before the full term of pregnancy. This results in the death of the foetus. Two key issues underpin Hindu views about abortion:

- **The sanctity of life**: Hindus believe that life is created by God and is therefore special. If a life is ended by abortion then this is a concern for some Hindus.
- **The law of karma**: Abortion could bring bad karma for the mother who makes this decision, as she has chosen to end a life. Although the soul of the child will be reborn, it has been denied this life now and so has been denied the chance to work through bad karma.

Hindus also believe the most traumatic times of life are conception, birth and death, so by aborting a foetus, it is being given only the traumatic aspects of life.

Hindu scriptures call abortion 'womb killing' and describe abortionists as the greatest of sinners. Gandhi, perhaps the most respected Hindu of the twentieth century, said: 'It seems to me clear as daylight that abortion would be a crime.'

However, abortion is legal in India and more than 5 million operations take place every year. For Hindus, having an abortion for reasons such as an unplanned pregnancy or social reasons is thought to be morally wrong. Any way of causing suffering to others is wrong.

In other cases, for example where the woman's life is at risk, then most Hindus would see abortion as acceptable. Also the pressure to have a son, but still to limit the family size, has encouraged some people to have abortions and take the karmic consequence. This is seen as an atrocity by many Hindus.

In any abortion the woman will gain bad karma for her actions. The key to just how much bad karma is determined by the intention behind her action – was she being selfish or thoughtless or cruel to break ahimsa, or was she trying to protect other lives? It is a moral decision, but religious beliefs shape that decision.

A foetus in the womb. In Hinduism, abortion is not considered to be a good thing.

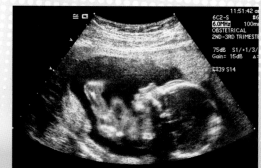

Euthanasia

Euthanasia is a gentle, easy death – helping someone to die because they are suffering and cannot get better. It is illegal almost everywhere in the world.

In India, it is common for people to leave their families so that they cease to be a burden, but it is not legal to help them die.

Most Hindus would say that a doctor should not accept a patient's request for euthanasia. This will cause the soul and body to be separated before it naturally should. This action will change the karma of both doctor and patient for the worse.

Other Hindus believe that euthanasia cannot be allowed because it causes suffering, for example to the families because they lose their relative. Simply put, it is wrong to take life, and euthanasia is exactly that – no matter why it is done.

However, some Hindus say that by helping to end a painful life a person is performing a good deed out of compassion (kindness), and this is a quality which Hindus should try to develop in themselves. For many Hindus, their conscience is their guide to such decisions.

Knowledge check

1 What is abortion?

2 What did Gandhi say about abortion?

3 What is euthanasia?

4 Why do most Hindus disagree with euthanasia?

Activity A

For each of the aspects of this topic (abortion and euthanasia), give reasons why most Hindus disapprove of those actions. Find out some Hindu teachings to support what you are saying.

Activity B

1 Explore teachings about the sanctity of life in Hinduism. Apply these to the issues of abortion and euthanasia.

2 Do these teachings make it acceptable or not to have an abortion, or take part in euthanasia? Explain your answer.

Activity C

In Hinduism, abortion is not considered to be a good thing, yet there are more than 5 million abortions a year in India. Can you work out the reasons why some people go against these teachings, and go ahead and have one (or more) anyway?

Activity D

Raj believes euthanasia is always wrong; Vashnie believes it is always acceptable. Both are Hindus.

1 How could they each defend their viewpoint?

2 Which teachings would support them in their views?

3.6 What does Hinduism teach about other faiths?

Learning objectives

You will … • find out about Hinduism and its relationship with other religions/faiths
• understand differences between Hindu, Buddhist and Sikh ideas.

Hinduism is the religion of the majority of people in India and Nepal. It also exists in significantly sized communities outside of India. It has over 900 million followers worldwide and it is the third largest religion.

Hindu believe that there are many ways to find God – like a mountain has many paths to the summit. There is no right or wrong way, all are equally valid. Yet relationships with other faiths have not always been smooth.

Dr Ambedkar on an Indian stamp.

Buddhism

Buddhism began in the north of the Indian subcontinent, and the Buddha himself was brought up in a Hindu tradition. Yet, after his enlightenment, the Buddha rejected the idea of God and the belief in a soul that passes from lifetime to lifetime. He emphasised that life was shared by all beings, and that all beings were equal. He therefore rejected the caste system.

In 1956, a 65-year-old Hindu leader called Dr Bhimrao Ambedkar converted to Buddhism. He was a Dalit – an Untouchable. He had struggled to get an education and improve the life he seemed destined to lead. He devoted much of his life to improving conditions for Dalits, and felt that Buddhist ideas about equality matched his own. He encouraged other Dalits to convert to Buddhism, and 500,000 of his followers did so. In 2006, 5000 Dalits converted to commemorate the 50th anniversary of Dr Ambedkar's conversion.

Knowledge check

Read pages 66–67.

1 Which countries are Hindu?
2 Why did Dr Ambedkar convert to Buddhism?
3 What was Operation Blue Star?
4 What was partition?

Sikhism

Sikhism began in India where Hinduism had already existed for thousands of years. As well as being a religion, Hinduism is a social way of organising people into groups – the caste system. Sikhism opposes this, believing that everyone is equal. This is shown by the meal called a langar, at which all are welcome at the place of worship, rich next to poor, including strangers.

Guru Nanak, the founder of Sikhism, was born into a Hindu family. He kept the Hindu ideas of **reincarnation** and karma, but he echoed Islamic beliefs of one God, and maintaining a relatively plain form of worship and a simple design of a holy building.

Sikhs in India have been persecuted. Many Sikhs want the state of Punjab to be independent from India. In 1984, India accused Sikh terrorists of hiding in the Golden Temple (the holiest Sikh place) in Punjab. In an action called Operation Blue Star, the Indian army stormed the temple and nearly 500 were killed – almost exclusively innocent Indian Sikhs.

Guru Nanak, the founder of Sikhism.

Islam

Islam came to India from the north west. It spread throughout the country, but was particularly strong in what is now Pakistan and Bangladesh. The Indian states there were ruled by Muslim leaders.

In 1947, India became independent from the British Empire and was partitioned (split) to create Pakistan as a state in its own right. Modern-day Bangladesh was East Pakistan until 1971. In the course of the partition, Hindus from Pakistan were forced into India, and Muslims from India into Pakistan. Communities were torn apart, and many died in fighting between the two religious groups.

Islam considers Hinduism to be a religion which worships idols, and so considers it wrong. This has led to many troubles between the two groups which continue today.

Activity A

An interfaith forum is a group of representatives of different faiths who meet to understand each other in a spirit of mutual respect. Using your knowledge of Hinduism and other faiths, design a logo for a local interfaith forum.

Activity D

1   Research one of the following: partition or Operation Blue Star.

2   Write an essay which explains to the reader the following about the option you have chosen to research:

   • What this was.
   • What happened.
   • Why it happened.
   • How the two sides have tried to move on from the issue.

3   In concluding your essay, make a judgement about the morality of it.

Activity B

Carry out Activity A. Now write a short piece to explain your design – what are the thoughts behind it?

Activity C

Partition resulted in the splitting up of India into countries based on religious make-up. Give reasons for and against this kind of an action.

The big assignment

Task

To design a set of individual postcards focusing on Hindu ethical issues.

Objectives

- To plan, design and colour a set of postcards on Hindu ethics.
- To research and provide information so that readers can learn about Hindu ethics.
- To self-assess the finished product.

Outcome

To produce a set of postcards (single or double sided) on Hindu ethics.

You should have done some research for images and prepared a text with focused information. You should include information about:

- karma
- ahimsa
- castes and poverty
- the environment
- animal rights
- abortion
- euthanasia.

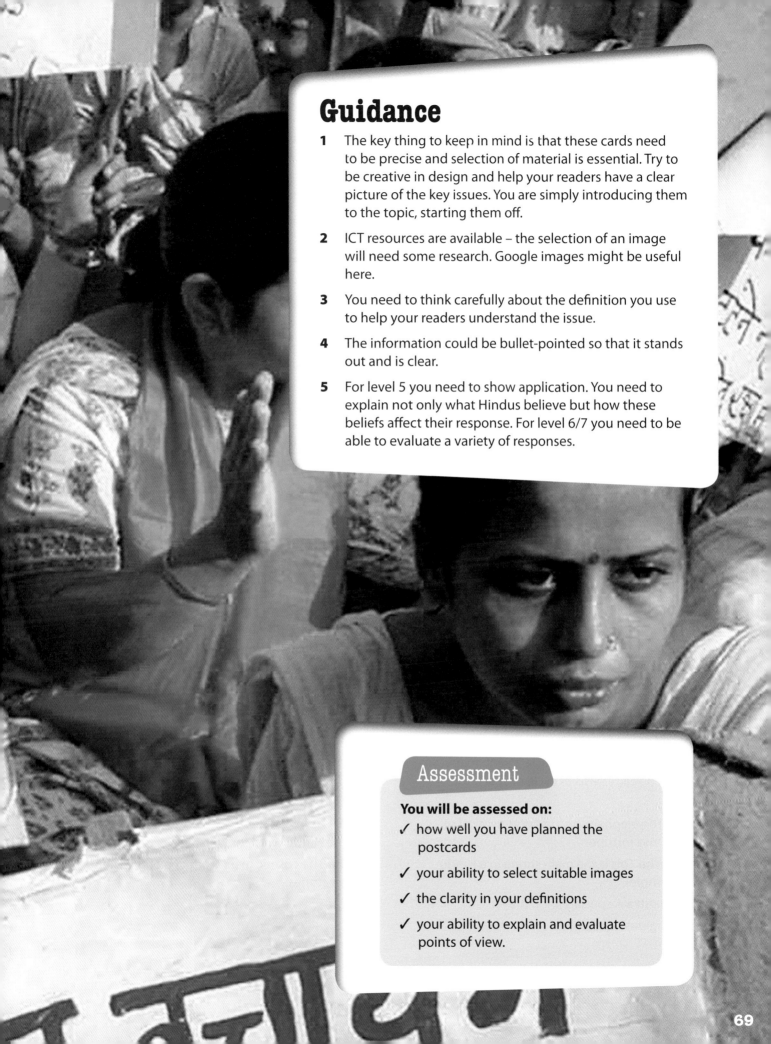

Guidance

1 The key thing to keep in mind is that these cards need to be precise and selection of material is essential. Try to be creative in design and help your readers have a clear picture of the key issues. You are simply introducing them to the topic, starting them off.

2 ICT resources are available – the selection of an image will need some research. Google images might be useful here.

3 You need to think carefully about the definition you use to help your readers understand the issue.

4 The information could be bullet-pointed so that it stands out and is clear.

5 For level 5 you need to show application. You need to explain not only what Hindus believe but how these beliefs affect their response. For level 6/7 you need to be able to evaluate a variety of responses.

Assessment

You will be assessed on:

✓ how well you have planned the postcards

✓ your ability to select suitable images

✓ the clarity in your definitions

✓ your ability to explain and evaluate points of view.

Glossary

Artha To earn money.

Arti A ceremony used to welcome the deity. It involves the use of light as a blessing.

Assisi Declarations These are statements made by each of the major world faiths about their attitude to the environment. These were made in a conference in 1986.

Atman The soul or spirit of an individual.

Aum (symbol) This is often chanted. The word is said to sound like the universe and the sound made when the universe was created.

Avatar Forms; the way gods appear on earth.

Bhajan Songs (hymns).

Brahma The god of creation and the first part of the Trimurti.

Brahman The name of God, the supreme spirit, the Ultimate Reality.

Caste Class or level/standing in society.

Dana Giving to charity.

Darshan Seeing the deity or holy person.

Daya Compassion.

Deity A Hindu god or goddess.

Diwali The Hindu festival of lights.

Duty Something a person has to do.

Epics Stories of the Hindu gods and goddesses.

Festival A celebration of a special event; many happen on a yearly basis or cycle of years.

Ganesha The elephant-headed god; symbol of good luck and fortune.

Garbha griha This is the main shrine in a Hindu mandir (temple).

Gayatri mantra A special Hindu prayer.

Guru A religious teacher.

Hanuman The monkey god who features in the Ramayana alongside Rama and Sita in their fight against evil.

Havan Sacred fire ceremony.

Holi A Hindu spring festival; celebrated with the throwing of waters and coloured powders.

Homophobia Prejudice against homosexuals.

Japa Meditation/prayer.

Karma Actions; the belief that good actions have good consequences, and bad actions have bad consequences.

Kirtan Mantras (chants).

Krishna A representation of Vishnu; his consort is Radha. They share spiritual rather than physical love.

Kumbha Mela A festival that takes place every twelve years.

Lakshmi The goddess of wealth and beauty and consort of Vishnu.

Mandir A Hindu temple.

Moksha To become one with God, having escaped the cycle of life.

Murti An image of god which helps worship – usually found on shrines in the mandir and at home.

Narasimha Vishnu in the form of half-man, half-lion.

Parikram Circling of the shrine.

Pilgrimage A sacred journey to special holy sites.

Prasad Offering and eating sacred food.

Pravachan Talk about the Hindu scriptures.

Puja The Hindu word for worship.

Purusha The cosmic giant from one of the Hindu creation stories.

Rama The hero of the Ramayana who is remembered at the festival of Diwali.

Ramayana The epic story of Rama and Sita – good versus evil.

Rangoli Intricate patterns traced outside houses at Diwali.

Ravana The ten-headed tyrant demon god in the story of Rama and Sita.

Reincarnation Rebirth of the soul.

Sacred Thread Ceremony A ceremony and celebration of the commitment for a Hindu boy.

Samsara The cycle of birth, life, death and rebirth.

Samskara Rites of passage; religious ceremonies that mark the stages of life.

Sanathan Dharma The preferred name for the Hindu religion. It means eternal law.

Sanctity of life Belief that life is precious and special.

Sewa Service to the deity or holy people.

Shiva The god of death, destruction and the recreation of life – the third part of the Trimurti.

Shrine An area in the temple or home that has the deity on it. The focus area for worship.

Shruti Teachings that 'were heard' from God and were passed on word for word.

Sita Wife of Prince Rama; symbol of loyalty.

Smriti Teachings that 'were remembered' of what ordinary people had been told about God. They are not the word of God.

Soul See atman.

Swastika Hindu symbol for good fortune.

Trimurti Three forms/images of God: Brahma, Vishnu and Shiva.

Varna See caste.

Vedas The most sacred of all scriptures – they are the word of God.

Vishnu The god representing preservation of life; the second part of the Trimurti.

Index